Fania's Heart

WRITTEN BY ANNE RENAUD
ILLUSTRATED BY RICHARD RUDNICKI

Second Story Press

Words have power.

There are words that injure and words that heal.

Then there are words that can save your life.

When I was young, my mother had many secrets.
Some she shared with me. Some she did not.
There was the secret of the tattooed number on her arm.
The secret of why she had no sisters, brothers, cousins, aunts, or uncles. And why I had no grandparents.
"They were swallowed up by a great darkness" was all she said.

When I was almost ten, I came upon another of my mother's secrets. I would have missed it had it not tumbled from a lace handkerchief I found in her dresser.

It was a tiny book shaped like a heart, no bigger than a butterfly. The cover was wrapped in purple cloth with the letter F embroidered in orange thread.

Each page opened like wings, revealing penciled writing inside. I struggled to read the words. Only here and there was I able to make out a few names. Ruth, Eva, Tonia....

Maybe Mama will tell me this secret, I thought. So I brought the heart to her. Mother was surprised to see the tiny book cupped in my hands. She sat down at the kitchen table and pulled me close.

"My sweet Sorale, this is a treasured gift," she said, tracing the embroidered letter with her finger as her brown eyes filled with tears. "The F stands for my name, Fania."

"Who made it?" I asked.

"This heart was made by brave young women who were like sisters to me. We came from different countries. Poland, Czechoslovakia, France, Belgium. Though we spoke different languages—Yiddish, Polish, French, German—we managed to understand each other. My best friends were Zlatka and Bronia. They were Polish, like me. Bronia, the eldest, watched over us like a mother. There were two French girls, Eva and Hélène. Then Hanka and Fela, Mina and Ruth. We were twenty friends in all—some only fifteen years old. We had all been torn from our homes and brought to the prison camp called Auschwitz," said my mother in a choked voice.

"You were in a prison?" I said, my eyes widening.

"It was wartime. Germany's Nazi army had invaded many countries in Europe. The leader of the Nazis, Adolf Hitler, hated certain people, especially Jewish people. He had concentration camps built where we were sent to be imprisoned or killed. We had done nothing wrong. We were in Auschwitz just because we were Jewish."

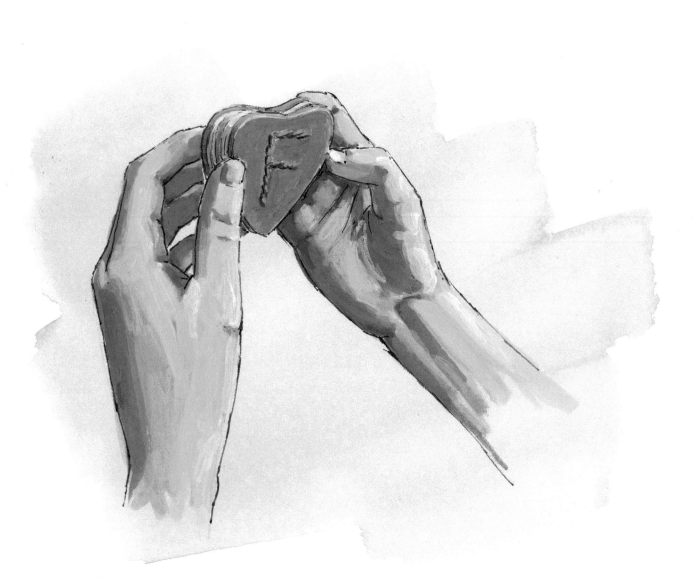

My mother went quiet for a while, and I stroked her hand. Then she sighed and went on.

"The tattoo on my arm—74207—is from that camp. We became numbers, no longer human beings.

We slept in our uniforms; gray and blue striped dresses. Every day, we woke in darkness to the bellows of guards. For breakfast, they gave us a cup of watered down coffee or tea. We stood outside for roll call, shivering in line sometimes for hours, while the chilly morning air covered us in goose bumps.

As the sun rose, we plodded through the camp gates, then along a dirt road until we reached a large factory building.

There, we were forced to make weapons for Hitler's army.

We did not want to make these weapons because we knew they would be used against the people who were trying to help us. We fought back in small ways. Sometimes we put dirt in the parts we made, or assembled them incorrectly, so they could not work.

We sat at long tables, ten of us on each side. We were forbidden to talk, forbidden to move from our benches. We worked for twelve hours, elbow to elbow.

Lunch was usually soup made from nettles and weeds. Because we were so hungry, we ate whatever was given to us. We had to eat if we wanted to survive. To keep from gagging, I would close my eyes and imagine my mother's chicken soup.

At dusk, we lined up outside the factory to be searched. The guards wanted to be sure we were not smuggling anything to use against them.

Exhausted, we then set off on the hour-long march back to camp. When it rained or snowed, our wooden shoes sank deep into mud, or slid on patches of ice. The guards were quick to whip or kick us if we stumbled and fell.

Evening meant soup again, this time flavored with potato or turnip peel. We also received our daily ration of bread, often stale or streaked green with mold. At night, we crowded into three-tiered bunks made of planks of wood. We slept four, five, and even six to a bunk, on a thin, lice-infested mattress with no pillow and one blanket to cover all of us.

I dreamed of my family: my older brother, Leybl, my younger sister, Moushka, and my dear mother and father. I prayed I would see them again. Every day, I searched for their faces among the other prisoners. But I never found them. I missed them so. I still do.

Over time, I learned to take comfort in the smallest things.

It was a good day when the rays of the rising sun warmed me and took away the chill as I marched to work.

I considered myself fortunate to be working in the factory. Indoors, we were not exposed to the numbing cold of winter or the scorching heat of summer. We had a better chance of surviving than the prisoners who worked outside, shattering rocks in a nearby quarry.

We all lived in constant terror of being beaten, of being shot. We were afraid of not surviving another day. But we coped as best we could.

Because we were always hungry, food was a favorite topic of conversation. We recited recipes to each other and imagined the day when we could eat to our hearts' content. There was little laughter, but we tried to make each other smile by telling funny stories.

As the months went by, we kept each other's spirits up with words of encouragement so we would not drown in our sad thoughts. With these women by my side, I never felt alone."

"But why did they make this heart for you?" I asked.

"You see, Sorale, one day I told my friends I would soon be an old lady, since my twentieth birthday was fast approaching."

"But twenty is not old," I said.

"Twenty can be a lifetime. We were all so worn and rope-thin. People did not live to be old in that place," said my mother.

"I did not imagine feeling any differently on my birthday than I had on all the days before. But I was wrong.

On the morning of December 12th, I sat at my work bench and noticed something being handed from one co-worker to the next and slowly making its way to me.

It was a small birthday cake my friends had pieced together from their precious bread rations.

They had remembered.

Tucked inside the bread was the heart you hold in your hands.

At first, I did not know what it was. I quickly hid it in my armpit so it would not attract the attention of the guards. Luckily they did not find it when they searched us at the end of the day.

That evening, when it was safe to whisper in our bunks, I opened the heart. It was then I realized it was a birthday card. Some messages were in languages I could not read, but my friends managed to convey what they had written.

Zlatka, whose idea it was to make the heart, explained how it came to be.

She had cut the cloth from her blouse, which I knew was her prized possession. She wore it underneath her striped dress, so the guards could not see it and take it away from her.

The glue used to put the heart together was made by mixing bread and water.

Zlatka and the others had to steal or barter the scissors, needle, thread, pencil, and paper in exchange for their meager food rations.

What a sacrifice! I remember thinking.

The heart needed to remain a secret. If the guards had found it, my friends would have been beaten or killed. They put their lives in danger by making this birthday card for me. They filled its pages with their courage.

That night I felt joy for the first time since I had arrived at the camp.
Every night that followed, I read the messages my friends had
written. Their words gave me strength and carried me through each
day until the war finally ended, and I was free once again."

"Can you read some of the messages to me? Please," I begged.

With great care, my mother unfolded the first page.

"These are written in Hebrew and Polish:

My beautiful Fania. A lot of luck and freedom, signed Giza.

May your life be long and sweet, signed Mazal.

I wish that all your wishes should be fulfilled, signed Irena.

This is my favorite message," said my mother, as she read from the fourth petal. "*Freedom, Freedom, Freedom,* signed Mania."

As my mother closed the tiny book, tears spilled from her eyes.

"This heart is all I can touch from my past. But it is not a sad heart. It is an act of defiance. A symbol of strength. An expression of hope and love. My friends wanted to prove that despite all that was inflicted upon us, we could still treat each other with humanity. Their words saved me."

Author's Note

In 1933, the National Socialist German Workers' Party, also called the Nazi Party, came to power in Germany. Its leader was Adolf Hitler, and its members were called Nazis.

The Nazis believed Germans were "racially superior" and that certain other groups of people were "racially inferior" and should be killed. Among those groups considered to be "inferior" were the physically and mentally challenged, homosexuals, Roma, Russian Polish, and in particular, Jewish people.

The Nazis' hatred toward Jews was reflected in increasingly brutal and oppressive laws. By 1945, an estimated six million European Jews had been killed by the Nazis. This genocide became known as the Holocaust.

Heart from Auschwitz

This story was inspired by Fania Landau Fainer, a Jew from Bialystok, Poland.

In January 1944, Fania arrived in Auschwitz with nothing more than the clothes on her back. She left the camp one year later, diminished and emaciated, and with only one possession; a heart-shaped birthday card, gifted to her by the women who worked with her in the Weichsel-Union Metallwerke. The "Union", as it was called by the more than one thousand prisoners, men and women, who labored there, was a munitions factory outside of Auschwitz.

The card was no bigger than a daisy and unfolded like an origami flower. Nineteen birthday messages were inscribed inside. Fifteen were written in Polish, one in German, two in French, and one in Hebrew.

In the weeks following her birthday, Fania, who slept in the middle bunk in her prison barrack, kept the heart hidden between the planks of wood that made up the bunk above her.

When Auschwitz was evacuated in January 1945, the birthday card traveled with Fania, tucked in her armpit as she trudged roads and rode cattle cars westward to Ravensbrück, the women's concentration camp in Germany. After the war, Fania made her way to Canada aboard the ocean liner *Aquitania*. Following her arrival at Pier 21 in Halifax Harbour on April 29, 1949, Fania settled in

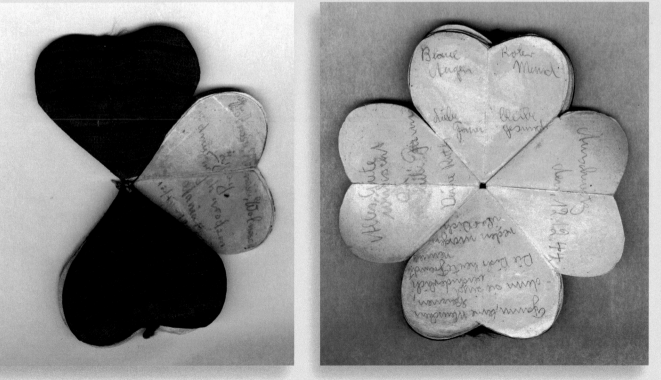

The front and back covers   *Open page from the heart from Auschwitz*

Toronto, after which her birthday card took up residence in her bedroom dresser.

In 1988, Krisha Starker, the director of the Montreal Holocaust Museum, and an old family friend, convinced Fania to donate the birthday card to the museum. Although it is one of the smallest pieces in the museum's collection, its message and impact are considerable. The heart is one of the few known objects to have been created by prisoners in Auschwitz.

Having lost everything in the war, it is also Fania's only material link to her past.

Fania Landau Fainer standing behind her heart
at the Montreal Holocaust Museum in 2010, at age 85.

In 2001, while visiting the museum, Montreal filmmaker, Carl Leblanc, was so moved by this relic he decided to search out the women who had signed the book. From this experience, he created a documentary film, entitled *The Heart of Auschwitz*, released in 2010.

Soon after liberation Fania met and married Aron Fainer, the love of her life, with whom she had two children and shared 60 wonderful years. Her daughter, Sandy (called Sorale as a child, a Yiddish name of endearment), her son, Harvey, her grandchildren, and great-grandchildren are her ultimate triumph.

Sandy (Sorale) age 9 in 1955, around the time she found her mother's heart-shaped birthday card.

"The Nazi project endeavored to destroy all sense of humanity in the people it targeted. The Heart from Auschwitz is resounding proof of the failure of this policy and of the persistence and strength of the human spirit."
— Montreal Holocaust Museum

Acknowledgments

Many hearts and hands went into making this book. A debt of gratitude is owed to the following people: Carl Leblanc, for sowing the seed; Fania Landau Fainer, who through unspeakable horrors remained unbowed and unbroken, for generously sharing her precious birthday card with the world; Sandy Fainer, for her unflagging support in helping me bring her mother's story to young readers; Cornelia Strickler, Education Coordinator, and Andréa Shaulis and Marie-Blanche Fourcade, Museum & Collection Coordinators at the Montreal Holocaust Museum, for their wisdom, guidance and the safekeeping of Fania's heart; and to the dedicated team at Second Story Press.

Dedication

For Fania, Hanka, Mania, Mazal, Hanka W., Fela, Berta, Mala, Ruth, Lena, Rachela, Zlatka, Eva, Bronia, Cesia, Irena, Mina, Tonia, Guta, and Giza, who found light even in the darkest of places.
—A.R

*To those whose lives were extinguished in the Holocaust, and to the brave survivors—
I am honoured to play a part in the telling of this story.*
—R.R.

Photo Credits
Page 28 and 29: Courtesy of the Montreal Holocaust Museum
Page 30: Courtesy of Ad Hoc Films
Page 31: Courtesy of Sandy Fainer

Library and Archives Canada Cataloguing in Publication
Renaud, Anne, 1957-, author
Fania's heart / by Anne Renaud ; illustrated by Richard Rudnicki.

ISBN 978-1-77260-057-5 (hardcover)

I. Rudnicki, Richard, illustrator II. Title.

PS8635.E51F36 2018   jC813'.6   C2017-906246-8

Text ©2018 Anne Renaud
Illustrations © Richard Rudnicki
Edited by Kathryn Cole
Designed by Ellie Sipila
Printed and bound in China

Second Story Press gratefully acknowledges the support of the Ontario Arts Council and the Canada Council for the Arts for our publishing program. We acknowledge the financial support of the Government of Canada through the Canada Book Fund.

Published by
SECOND STORY PRESS
20 Maud Street, Suite 401
Toronto, ON M5V 2M5
www.secondstorypress.ca